ALSO BY PHOEBE WANG

Admission Requirements

Waking
Occupations

Phoebe Wang

McClelland & Stewart

McClelland & Stewart and colophon are registered trademarks of Penguin Random House Canada Limited.

Published simultaneously in the United States of America.

Library and Archives Canada Cataloguing in Publication data is available upon request.

ISBN: 978-0-7710-9939-7
ebook ISBN: 978-0-7710-9940-3

Book design by Jennifer Griffiths
Cover image: *Skyline of Cranes in Yaletown* by John Wang
Typeset in Aldus by M&S, Toronto
Printed in Canada

McClelland & Stewart,
a division of Penguin Random House Canada Limited,
a Penguin Random House Company
www.penguinrandomhouse.ca

1 2 3 4 5   26 25 24 23 22

Penguin
Random House
McCLELLAND & STEWART

Night Scene for a Revoked Citizen   3

I. PARTINGS

II. STILL LIVES

III. BRIEF ENCOUNTERS

IV. WITHOUT ELEGIES

Waking Occupations

In a dissolving country I petition for entry.
The sky slides to pitch and the moon goes grainy
over cloud counties   crown lands
over insubordinate shores slivered into portions
and sun-hewn roads where I've walked until my legs
renounced me. I'm tired with doubleness.
There, between scrub pine and dock pilings,
the water is a wiped slate   a temporary respite.
But I have no birthright here, no chain of title.
Fireflies patrol the woodshed, tender dogs rave
at my vagrancy. They take my blood scent,
take payment. I tender the yellow leaves, the last heat,
and jettison my attachment to terra firma,
my body's wayward boat expecting betrayal.
Knees kowtow to the cold cured mud
and my breath submerges, parallel to bedrock.
I glide into solace like a selkie into her real clothing.
Some nights, each stroke is an embrace in reverse,
carrying me halfway across placating currents.
The warmth amniotic.   The heart beats its animal kettle.
Other nights, I'm escorted like a hostage, tethered
to the shallow places, the perimeters, and never loosened
to the centre where desire can unfold beyond
its cross-examinations. Ahead, the horizon
is irreproachable and mapless, its mouth accumulating
rafts, bribes, toll payments. Every night is a bartering.
Time's accounting doesn't slow, but I recover
in the absence of stars for one rotation, until, then . . .

the unperforated dark, the ash-black, bone-black,
iron-black, outer edges flaming like surface corrosion,
streaking to vermillion   the blood glow through skin.
Light drags me through an aperture,
publishes me on the filmy paper of renewal,
and I am admitted on a trial basis into a merciful heat,
into a generous blankness   into the caesura of myself,
dripping with ink and dispossessions, to infiltrate
the site of resuscitation   of mending
of every alarm sounding   of irreversible exile
where my transgressions and flightless status
are cauterized in a country I wake to recover.

I. PARTINGS

for THE SPLIT SELF

Why do I cling to it, that shadow country,
it was a veil, kind and warm as linen,
but easily cleaved.   When I open my eyes
the chimera dissipates   in autumnal light
and though its single version of events was not
the legacy I presumed   it was pleasant there
with official rhetorics.   I would've remained
had not my body evacuated me from the mind's
stateless borders, its collapsing vestibules.
I'd been aware of a patchiness, a thinning
in the opacity, in the white noise generator,
in well-meaning intentions and loopholed treaties.
For one thing, I wasn't a match for my surroundings,
my skin in quiet revolt   my face a murmur.
But I've had enough of being neither here nor there,
prone as a fish between the coming wave
and a comatose citizenry. How weary it is to be
a deportee of a dismantled aftermath. What it costs.
I rise as a rupture   with that passive woman,
bathed in golden light yet insisting this is no day
of tumult, that I have no role in the bell-tolled world,
that I have no protocols or heralds of parting.
The systems are not broken. No alarm is sounding.

for PERMANENT RESIDENCE

What if it could be measured, the tumbling
into the quick river of sleep—what unit
of length or force or weight? I couldn't discern
its creeping lassitude, its soft coercions.
When the lodestone tipped off my chest
my body began its protocol of resuscitation.
I surface with easier syllables yet still on trial.
The ceiling and cold floors agree this is no birthing
but a repackaging for another kind of servitude.
I listen to the doublespeak of the news,
omniscient with its undertow of *them* and *us*.
How long have I been buoyant as foam,
floating and unreconciled to split histories?
I didn't know it was possible to wake engulfed.

for BREAKING NEWS

The news hadn't yet arrived, but it was in transit.
My mother woke, and urged the rest of us to reach
the same inevitability, her *wei, hai sun-ah*!
like the kick of an engine. Our future was labelled and due
to arrive on the back of the truck in orange boxes
wedged between September sun and timetable blocks.
The house was rented and empty of suspicions.
It had its own agenda, and did not concern itself
with what we were unpacking. I evicted sleep
while passengers somnolent miles above us
were startled by sudden turbulence, a windshift.
We'd resolved on a peeling bungalow, a salt-licked city.
The resolution was a projectile. It could be hijacked
by windstorms, by a request, by anything really.
Did you hear? The movers asked, but the means of hearing
hadn't reached us, hadn't yet been unpacked.
The earliest messengers flashed beacons to signal
the strength of the enemy. A woman composed a text
in the stairwell of a burning building. Twenty years later
we're dazed by the flare of dispatch.

for AN OCCASIONAL EMERGENCY

We had stable conditions until we didn't.
It's dangerous to presume on a level plane, but forgivable.
What kind of treachery is it to wake inverted,
plaster in our mouths, the bed a wayward raft,
limbs sliding groundward, tumblers askew?
When warnings come, we're sleep-enclosed,
insentient to cloudy stars, the city rumbling
like a bad stomach, sulphur streaking the horizon.
Playgrounds are bisected by yellow tape,
offices hollowed by vaporized orders. We wake
to the walls' new arrangements, new anatomies.
We wash the dust from our eyelids and venture
out under shelves of sky, scavengers of belief.

for THE TRANSIENT

Not knowing how far or how fast we're moving
nonetheless there's solace or an equivalent within the belly
of the warm and rumbling vehicle lifting us
past river fragments and farmland with no will left.
If we were ferried past a border in the night, we can't recall
what was exacted. It's too soon to miss our nightstands,
our faults of housework, our names in mellow refrain.
Because our sleep twisted restlessly back on itself
like a moth uncertain of its path, we forget our gratitude
at being temporarily freed from the decision-making.
Our waking is less like driving a stake into new earth
than it is a flustered leaf relenting its weak hold.
We capitulate to stale attention, to our seatmate struggling
to his feet, to the cramp loyal to our necks and tendons,
because by now, fallow land gives way to torn asphalt,
and loose silvery rain soothes us with its understanding.
Today will contain reports of mismanagement
from higher-ups, routes no longer serviced,
geese overhead, portents of a shuttered season,
and at last, the inexplicable way you're greeted
at the station, enfolded into the ridges and valleys
of someone's soap-soft, animal smell, accepting
every door you left burning, every pillar of salt.

INTERLUDE WITH FIGURES IN PASSING

after Over Vitebsk, Marc Chagall, 1914

There is the country that accepts our bodies
on washed cotton, that logs our hours in blue columns.
There is another that arrests our spectres
so we cross over without the weightless drag
of wounded villages and streets sunken with ordnances.
What half-remembered dream persecutes our sleep?
Even the stars are packing up and moving houses.
We're night-walkers cordoned by a gauntlet of pine
that lines highways   creeks   then a clear strip
between properties   waymarked by eagle feathers
half-buried in the drifts. There's no way of knowing
when we reach the border   there's no demarcation
no white beacons   no guardhouse   so we keep flying
over rooftops and nacreous church domes
our suitcases stuffed with wool scarves and paper.
We make no tracks nor collude in acts of forgetting.
The night keeps no files.   We submit applications
to heavy-lidded windows and drowsy bells.
We submit our children tied with red string.
The townsfolk dream of running ahead of us
to ready our beds. They smile with closed mouths,
saying, *whatever you are fleeing, we have also fled.*

for THE GOOD INTENTIONED

The light doesn't accuse me.
Still I'm held accountable to dark acts
that unravelled in muffled corridors
when my back was contracted
in sleep and my faculties occupied with chimeras
of houses shared, of a lakeside property
where we look for movement in the cattails.
I let go too easily, like a bit of milkweed,
drifting off to other, misappropriated lands,
where the only deviation between being here and there
is how richly hued my consignments of care,
chalk white, eggshell stucco, emergency red,
legal pad lemon, dismissive black of signatories.
So I succeed to that redacted file, that averted gaze,
mine to unravel with my citizen's unrest.

for MEETING OBLIGATIONS

Enough of putting off the inked light. I slip
in and out of the early hours like a smuggler
through the patrols, with my cargo of smoke and cedar.
I will commit to the breath that brings a whiff of earth,
of rot, of lavender, of my sweat and trepidation,
and trade that holding place for light's impartial fingers,
for the weight of linen, for the close air, greasy with sleep,
for a mouth papery with thirst. A place beyond
known ports, salt-lashed and groaning,
shirts scattered over foam, snagged on rail fences . . .
Now I levitate, crack my ankles, and register discomforts
with the magistrates of my body. I use as leverage
the recognizable forms, the soft envelope of the room,
the mirror sure of its purpose to keep giving back.
I will get back to you. I see the flashing notifications—
the upcoming appointment with the Japanese maple,
the student waiting in the corridors of her intention,
the message about your mother's weak heart.
There is the thread about our collective action.
There are growlings to be addressed.
But I've lost feeling in my left foot. I tell myself,
time to clothe yourself in tacit agreements,
to put your arms through the stretched openings.
There was a time when I thought of my knees
and they obeyed. I thought of music and I was singing.
I thought of rain and was soaked in its high stakes,
and I was weather too, with shifting conditions,
indifferent to shelter and ditches and magnificence.

for A VENEER OF PROGRESS

When I concede a fictional country, I gain a battleground,
wake stunned as if under attack   and come to relearn
the architecture of my sloughed-off clothing, my uniform
of striped shirts and rigid black jeans   splayed books,
unagitated water glass, brass and silver chains
fastening light to the wall, holding it accountable.
Another time I rose from a rush mat on the floor,
fastened myself into hooks and eyes   heard myself
named by honorific   nonexistent from the record of harvests
except as a handprint in dust   an unscripted drama.
Another time I masked as a boy and vanished to sea.
So this morning that is a rupture   is a gain of sorts
though the body is still contested   under ribbed occupation
and to rise under the deadweight of progress
is to unlatch myself   from soft, enveloping creases
is to overcome the paralysis of productive time   while enfolding
in my collars and eyelids   acts of sleepless refusal.

for A MILLENNIUM

At dawn, sparrows counting their numbers, by the dozens, thousands.
Or your dogs reminding you with damp noses you're the beholden one.
Your neighbour's three-year-old tumbling above for the joy of it.
Workmen swearing on the roof, you forgot this was the day of tarring.
A child's heat against your collarbone. An axe emptying itself
on the chopping block. The chime of milk bottles on the front step.
A hand reaching for your soft waist, turning you to pleasure or need.
The radio leaping with The Drifters, KC and the Sunshine Band,
Men at Work, Dire Straits. A bugle sounding reveille. Bells shaking
the town square. Your phone shuddering like an oversized insect.
An apologetic rain through the blinds. *Just once in my life,*
sighs Anna of Downton, *I'd like to sleep until I woke up natural.*
You rive your eyelids to your grandmother already making
the dry straw glow, the thread of smoke rising to the rafters.
A messenger who has run all night through wild parsley
and the day is given to rejoicing and naming the fallen.

for A TEMPORARY ENCAMPMENT

The Encampment, Fort York, 2012

The last night we lit effigies of scrap wood.
We had no confirmation that the spirits
could hear us but we drank and lay side-by-side
in our sleeping bags on the indifferent earth.
Our fellow collaborators danced
across our canvas tents like crooked puppets
until embers crumbled into the night.
We succumb to a measure of peace of mind,
the protection afforded by our collaborators.
Our sleep wanders the barracks, stumbles
over earthworks and brambles, and smelling the lake,
rolls under the Gardiner towards the breakwater.
We wake to the vapour of rain through tent flaps.
Dismantling our watch, we bundle it onto our backs,
pull the plugs out of soft ground and collapse
the unbleached fabric like skin without bones to hold it up.
Soon it will be winter and our campaigns impassable.
The old fort has been the site of another battle.
Our mornings are conscripted. We move
through the village with its streets and alliances,
discharging our civilian inclines.

You could be forgiven for wanting a return to unknowing
like the silky seeds that cleave to the split pod,
fearful of the four directions. For years you've been carried
from what you've always known to what's beyond
the edge of the trees, where the gravel road tapers
into a footpath, and though you haven't trekked there
yourself, others have marked the way with spray paint
and footprints in the softened ground. This way, now.
You've roamed these hills for years without seeing
the perimeter or the smudged faces below the cliffs,
the women who disappear from concession roads.
In the morning, you shake dead flies from the screen door
and swim towards stalled freight trains, barricades,
to relieve your sleepless kin defending our lifelines.

for THE DELIRIOUS

Dark wings on my pupils. A lamp in my core
is burning up the bedposts and my cotton nightie
and the splayed paperbacks and the calendar
with its categorical divisions. They secured me
when I served them with non-essential labour,
muted myself on entering, assessed performances.
Now the noons and blue evenings have unlatched
and let in the fever birds into my cloistered room.
The bed is a holding pen, and there is freedom
in its stretched aubade, its perimeter of heat.
My infected attitudes will not spread as long
as my flushed state is a pretext for missing
mealtimes and morning buses. I am washed
in nightsweats. The window condenses in sympathy.
My illness has stretched years, decades, perhaps
has always lingered in my inboxes, my chained
agreements, the casual contracts of my breath.
When I rise, the earth will bear a reduced load.
I will shake free of the cleaving bequests
and the embrace of my prone and weaker half.

for INSOMNIACS

What if I'm never released into the indigo,
dip-dyed shoreline of sleep,
but remain marooned on arid knolls
to barter with the ferrymen of hope?
And what if I hadn't met you,
or heard your raucous laugh, been subject
to your assessing gaze across your living room,
across its electric currents and whirlpools?

Then we might have had some relief, some rest.
Tomorrow is another day we won't meet.
So I continue my sorting through the shredded
nylon knapsacks of assignments,
soggy agendas, rubrics of restitution.
Somewhere among the rubbish and rocks cauled
in moss are our bodies, sealed like bunkers.
Here, your breathing says, *over here.*
Mornings your msgs bubble up like confessions.

for A LONG DISTANCE

If you were here, you wouldn't disturb me.
Last night's ice-storm pillaged
the maples of their remaining foliage,
but by morning, the cracked powerlines,
the gloss of ice, are as much a part of the landscape
as the neighbourhood's silvery sage or patio set.
What I mean to say is, something caused by force
could, with time, become tolerable and domestic.
It's not that you deny me, but let it be known
we have been victims of an excess of caution,
to the logistics of prevention. The story goes,
my great-grandfather left behind a foreign lover.
The story goes, they didn't see their first wives
for so long that in their husbands' eyes
they remained young as pearls newly exposed
to air and light, unpierced and unstrung.
I have been the point of departure, like the women
before me, but now we take turns.
We will have to pay for our re-emergence,
they are fond of taxation here. It will cost
an easier story filled with scraps and straw
and newspapers and feathers and spread over me
to the edges of my bed and property.

for THE TRANSIENT #2

I give my name to the concierge in exchange
for nights of blank coolness, quenching as sparkling water.
I've earned a reprieve of anonymity, the snag of a stranger's glance

across the marbled lobby, which I appreciate for its lack
of pressed history. That is a kindness bestowed to travellers,
and I stretch out on its expanse as on hundred-count cotton.

I bang my elbows on armchairs, on their harmless set-up.
My role exacts a fierce concentration. Each day I collect
sights and sounds, and return with a permissive weariness.

Here I'm a reduced woman, adding up what the day cost,
the bus fare, the souvenir guide, the strange phrases, the skyline,
the masked children, the woman selling moon-folded pastries in the park.

Beside me, other guests close and open drawers,
vibrating like small aftershocks, and laughter in the hall
reaches me through a tunnel. Curtains of white noise pull

over the room, and I slide off the ledge of wakefulness, as if walking
absentmindedly into vapour. Hours or days or moments later
I'm hauled toward a sonorous pulse,

through layers of fuzz and linen until reaching
for firm plastic I hear my name released back to me,
the name that rehearses, that apprehends, that indicts.

for AN IMMINENT DEPARTURE

The morning before, and the morning before that one,
I waited for permission to leave my habitual latitudes.
There was resistance, of course, binding me
with appointments, fine gold chains,
soon-to-expire yogurt, and an invisible peril
to the constructions and estates of the real.
My absence could be manifested by hums
and murmurs, cold lightbulbs forgetting their wattage,
sinks going parched as mouths without tongues, or else
by a hand I didn't take, a table I didn't reserve,
a chlorine furlough, tinted robin's egg-blue, I never
crawled through. My alarm increases its exhortations.
Our lovers ceased their pleas for us to tarry.
The waiting became the journey. I didn't deny
the dawn, but neither did I evacuate.

for THE IMMUNE

The trick is, how to be patient as a window.
Numb on one side, compensating on the other,
double-paned, with a vacuum of air in between.
How to lie flat and still in quiet, fallow,
dreaming of what will enter me.
How to maintain divisions between seasons
of violence and the weather within.
Always the threat of exposure. The hard stare
of the shrinking sun, the menace clinging
to surfaces. I should keep close to my marked walls,
but it's too much effort to be immune and distant
from fragrant trees, from the transient beauty
of moonlight and silver foam, and to wait for lakes
to visit and for herds to regain their wholeness.

II. STILL LIVES

Behind the glowing door, its blank motives,
a woman sits at a scarred table, implements in hand.
The silence is a kind of weather.

She woke up with it, dressed in its chill folds.
The door is never shut. There's a glint of light
beneath it and I creep across navy carpet,

through reeds and underbrush, cracked highways,
parched streams, through years in deficit to where
she leans over the prerogative of making.

I hear the paintbrush chime against glass, the chair creak,
the plunge of her concentration. The hinges
don't mention my approach as I disclose

her thin back, her bobbed hair, the window filled
with weak clouds and tedious houses,
dusk applied with a wet obscuring wash.

She is drawing from life without its interruptions,
without weeds or toys in the grass. She distills.
I look over her shoulder.

Now the chair is empty as a podium.
I can refuse it, the way I've shunned lead outlines
and lucid pigments. But not the invitation

into wider rooms than the one I occupied,
the old growth opening alluringly onto the valley,
that scissor of sun through the birch, unrepentant.

STILL LIFE WITH ALLEGORICAL INTENT

Beyond the finite edge of the snowy, mould-made paper
and the afternoon closing like movie credits,

she hears with a buried ear the key shifting the bolt,
the cheerful feet on the stairs, the tap sighing,

her daughters climbing towards that part of her
that can be summoned out of a makeshift studio.

She comes back to us not like a wayfarer, breathless
with recounting, but speechlessly, disinclined

as a gardener in congealed, bone-dry season
to acquaint us with harshness. We begin to guess

that there's a lesson in the way her back is turned to us.
That divisions are inevitable as doorways.

And yet wherever she has been, she returns seamlessly,
rising from the stern black chair, as if it were an easy thing

to rinse her attention from its demands,
as if it were usual to stalk asymmetry and grace

with pools of sepia and gum arabic, to be a wedge
between a starved life and a saturated one.

As if she were making an argument, not for beauty,
but for yellow tulips supple with purpose,
the patternless patina of a brass kettle, while the hand
that arranged them is suggested in the gathering
of dusky blueberries, apples turned towards
the light, or away from it, the source of which is unseen.
And yet, beauty persists, because of what has been
removed so that each bundle of straw, each arrangement
could be presented without rot or browning
and that persistence bled beyond the negative spaces
to our living room, the fruit in their wooden bowl,
the patchwork quilts on our single beds, until it was all
I could see, along with her bent efforts.
No, not an effort, but a will to remake the world
to convince us it was preferable to the real thing,
could fill the blanks on walls that were wanting.

NUDE WITH WHITE SPACE

after Walasse Ting's Woman with Flowers, 1977

Every morning a woman wakes wanting
is a dry brush dragged across baleful canvas.
Until she's not flesh anymore, not a dark furor
of hair or the whites of eyes, but an assemblage,
tidier than a terrain viewed in passing
when outlines blur and run, getting away from us,
distilled to essentials. The foreground colludes.
The in-between hours are restless squiggles,
the cleft between the crook of elbow and bare
torso is a blind alley, a closed cove.
The inverted triangle between her legs
is a wine glass, an abyssal plain slowly dropping.
Viewed from afar, her body is rendered
in relief, into knowable routes, and we can allege
here is where she begins, here is where we've been.
Yet I want some part of her unconquered,
unconquerable. That flood meadow,
glassy after freezing rains, too contained and whole
onto itself for us to even think of traversing it.

Until she conjured her own house my mother lived in a palette
of wheat and alpaca, Mennonite butter and patchwork florals.
Her hair undiluted ink, glistening under her first snowfall.
Because mine is as heavy as hers, I can profess her story as my own.
Children are blank canvases, primed for a landscape of succour.
I slept between pastures sealed like a block of cold pressed paper,
embossed with the indelible edges of what followed us here.
When I woke, the shaking house, its hand-me-down wicker
and sandalwood drawers with creased, red-seamed hurts
were softer, more acceptable. I had the impression of digging
myself from papery layers of forgetfulness. Her tongue slow
to wake, my mother stirred oatmeal, fried eggs, spilled soy sauce
like a signature into our bowls, then described last night's dream,
the heaving back of sea and sky, grey-green, wide as a film.
Certain things I couldn't digest, others I adopted a tolerance for:
the placid sweetness of milk, mayonnaise that clots the throat.
When my sister and I were stuck on fish bones translucent as belief
we were told what they'd been told, to swallow mouthfuls
of rice until the weight of the grains pushed down the threat.
When there were parts of the paper she wanted untouched
my mother applied liquid mask and later, rubbed it away to reveal
a highlight, a place for the gaze to rest, a future not coloured in.

STILL LIFE WITHOUT SEPARATIONS

after Matisse, Goldfish and Sculpture, 1912

Without hesitation she climbs in
and when she winces we feel it too.
The surface plunges her calves, her thighs,

then the tract of her tummy into bloom,
a deep vermillion. It'll do the same to us,
when we slough off cotton socks and tank tops,

climbing in as if into a second skin,
first my sister, then me. We fit beside
our mother like her own, slippery fins.

We're contained within the jade-green tub,
within the frame. Our voices blend together
on the blue tile, giggles spill over the rim.

There's no separation between the heat
outside our bodies and that we hold in.
The light amniotic. Even when we're clean

we don't climb out. We could live here,
in a dance of chiaroscuro, rinsed in cerulean.
Outside the window the air is frigid and hostile.

But her moments were tropical.
I gaze at three goldfish in a room of orange,
acanthus green, chromatic earth, and a woman alone

in repose. We don't expect anything different,
Mom passes us a washcloth, a white pill of soap,
gives us no choice but to use them.

STILL LIFE FOR THE MYTH OF ORIGINS

after Modigliani's Jeanne Hébuterne, 1919

The banyan tree beside the battered pier didn't ask questions,
neither did the sleeping dogs.

In the aura of the reddened trees, my great-grandfather
is strolling. He's been away, a few years, maybe more,

given the distance by steamship those days, the greater distance
of pitched tones into elongated accents,

so his return is not to the place where he embarked.
My great-grandfather wipes his brow

as he walks through the village in a padded coat,
two freckled, amber-eyed children in tow. So goes the story.

The story drifts down like strains of a French song from a window
caught by my mother, standing below in her school dress.

The records were scratched, and she didn't understand
their passionate affairs: *Vous savez bien*

que dans le fond je n'en crois rien—I can't explain her penchant
for brie and baguettes, the name she gave herself, or

why she landed in a country where
she'd always have an accent.

She began a self-portrait but took years to fill in the outline
of a woman with hair like a wave, a colourless stare.

Lately only my dad knows her as Hau Yee.
The old village men were still shuffling mahjong tiles

in the sea-blown square when my mother returned
with a daughter in one arm and another beside her.

She tells the story often. The men hadn't changed
position. They called to us, seeing the resemblance.

STILL LIFE WITH DREAM INTERPRETATION, #2

After Lu Shou Kun's (呂壽琨) Zhuangzi is Free, 1974

Another night
my mother is flying,
an old wish fulfilled,

and below,
the islands of her discontent and youth,
territories knotted together by bilateral agreements.

From the height of her middle age,
her solid four-poster bed,
she pinpoints herself splayed on her narrow upper bunk,
in dormitories where girls slept squeezed as soldiers.

Floor supervisor by sixteen, she overfilled her quota.
Eligible bachelors waited for her by the factory gates
to escort her to the Royal Theatre or to Yau Ma Tai for dessert,
her curtained hair swaying, sandals slapping wet asphalt
after a prosperous rain. The air clammy with fish stalls
and riotous with housewives tottering down from aerial views
she was meant to have.   The one she wakes to
is closer to land   alight   free of premonition.

The quality of silence, the fine, toothy grain of it,
snowlight through glass.

The dining table, varnished, indented where knots
couldn't be smoothed out, and the cane rattan seats.

My sister and I, our feet dangling, sweatshirted,
our brows drawn like parentheses.

We confront the blown-up image, sunflowers,
Cezanne's bright oranges, divided into quarters

like territory to be conquered, one square inch at a time.
Dad's in a polo shirt, glasses with wide frames.

He gestures to the distraught brushstrokes,
the tumbled compositions. Mom sets us up

with plastic palettes, sets of synthetic (cheaper than sable)
short-handled brushes. She's a background figure,

bobbed hair with reddish undertones.
She gives us more or less equal amounts

of cadmium like a bloody sun, lemon yellow kind
as a pep talk, hues culled from chemical,

iron, clay, madder, bone that'll be dirtied
and flecked before we're done.

Then the looking, looking up, looking over
at the direction of light, back to the underlayers

of taupe and expectation. I mixed the quiet
until it was bright and laid it in loose dabs.

As the hours dried out I got up to survey
my canvas at a distance, at what I hadn't met.

The walls are not bare even when they're bare,
even when they're newly plastered and nacreous white,
they burn on winter mornings.

While heavy with her firstborn
my mother awoke amid that blankness, in a blank capital
with cauterized wounds, among neighbors of uncertain entrances.

My father rises before her,
sits up from under their mortgaged lives.
They have installed themselves like eyehooks, waiting

for the weight of all that will hang from them:
rosewood chests, fireworks, Christmas trees, college diplomas,
highchairs, birthday cakes, Milk Calendars, sponsored brothers.

He pulls on his long johns in the dark.
It's January, not yet light, a pale glow washing
the snow-heaped yard and my mother's eyelids.

She untangles herself from a dream of islands
wrapped in haze. She's still heavy with the leave-taking.
She rises to stir cream into quick oats,

the stovelight resting on her belly,
on thin fingers that do fine, pen-and-ink lettering,
that turn the lock after her husband swims out into the drifts.

After, she'll curl back under the womb of quilts
to sleep in a house laid out according to a custom plan,
so devoid of doors its stirrings and energies

will circle the wood floors and the bits
of wicker furniture until with a hot rush
they burst through the watery film stretched to break.

The vault is cool as a grotto.
I descend into eggshell, mineral tunnels
that open into carved chambers

where crimson images flash
in feeble light. Here are the lessons.
There are lessons in shade and tone and value.

Lessons in highlights and how they sharpen
when a dark hue is adjacent.
I'm still using that trick, placing objects

in oblique relation to each other.
Steamed bass on a blue patterned plate.
Our black bobbed hair under stovelight.

Against the flat backdrops of dinnertime
Dad leaps up the basement stairs like a spark,
a still-wet canvas in hand, needing us

to be on equal terms with his enthusiasm.
Presses us. Will not let us depreciate.
Picasso, Dad proclaims, painted

his sister Lola as his first exhibition piece
to confirm to his teachers what he'd mastered.
Picasso, always Picasso. Dad enumerates the difficulties:

the candlelight, the brass filigree lamp, the lace
over the altar boy's red tunic, that sheerness
with the colour staining through.

The library books slide to the floor, so heavy
they flatten dissent. We lower our gazes
to our servings of fish and doggedness as Dad repeats—

Picasso's father himself an art teacher, and so, you see—
the lesson is regret and regret is droning,
in intonations so thick

it made a groove wide enough
for a calling, for a border crossing,
for a revolt, for a track through a whitened vista.

Our parents flip between the same few channels.
There's the *if only my father had done the same*
and the *you don't know how lucky you are.*

Half-paying attention, my sister and I pretend
to be elsewhere, but we're helpless
to the guise, the make-believe.

Mom rents them by the armfuls
and we rewind the videotape, another ruffled
fantasy of a model-turned-mistress. The machine whirls

as my sister wonders if Camille really helped herself
to marble boulders Rodin's gang
left by the wayside.

If she cracked the roles she was cast in,
muse and madwoman, if her life melted out
like lost wax? Mom's forehead is dense as granite

as she knits to the end of the row, turns it, starts again.
She too makes good use of discards
and sticky materials,

of a lower set of standards.
She switches between vehemence and doubt,
insisting that anything worth doing is worth doing well.

She tsks at our charcoal-smudged shirts, our repulsion
of symmetry. Very little escapes her.
Imitation would lift us beyond her reach.

My sister's boyish, stick-man figure
is the same as our mother's no matter how much
they help themselves. Her running joke

about the probability of dying young
from TB doesn't amuse me.
This isn't the 19th century.

But count how many, she says, Tchaikovsky,
Kafka, Modigliani. We ride the bus to art school
past ashen mock-Gothic and low-rises afflicted

with utilitarianism. Our olive skin
takes on a sickly pallor. Chopin, The Brontë sisters,
Stravinsky. She declares I'm like Charlotte, she, Emily,

alienated not by distance but by malady.
We show no other symptoms
of genius. I imagine it as a savage wind

harassing a Yorkshire moor, knocking at the panes
of a smoky garret, searching for a body
to invade. But it won't find us.

Nearly women, we pack our bags in quest
of a novel idea, a rented room, a shadeless lamp
to carve angles where they're none.

Other points of departure are the foreign scenes
we made by the picturesque mill,
picnicking with cha-shu bao and lemon tea.

Our parents sensitive
to stray gazes, to the whites of eyes.
I told them they were just imagining things.

We set no precedents except by being
hungry for colour, by not being content
with buying chestnuts and lotus roots in Chinatown

or with doing everything we could find to do for free
in our neck of the woods, our prudent capital
with its newly cast National Gallery.

In vast, impersonal hallways we greet
Claude, Paul, Auguste and Vincent like old friends.
People turn to look. Impulsively our mom drags us

onto trains, road trips away from our wakings
with the same northern sun skating across
our bleached walls, towards budget

hotels and delis in metropolises
where we could be nameless and jostled
by grander sensations and louder mornings.

Our parents give us no clue what to expect
when they steer us to the liquid edges
of Monet's *Water Lilies* at the Met.

We stood ankle-deep, soaking in its volume,
its lessons of monumental scale,
in how a bounded view

of lilies knit close as a tribe,
local skies immersed in stretched reflections,
could present an endless illusion.

At sixteen I slip into romantic notions
like a willow limb into the canal,
reaching for saturation.

I set up wobbly water-ringed tables
where the Refused lounge in frock-coats
sharing the tracts of their discontent.

They slap the warped surfaces until they quake,
talking of what provisions, what approach to take.
At dawn, they trek beyond

the grand boulevards and wade waist-deep
en plein air, into heather and meadow-rue,
into light already changing its mind.

I begin planning my own expedition,
through the reeds to a carved shoreline,
already captured in small, unsatisfactory pieces.

I lack the broad shoulders to force through
the profuse incredulity, to rove uninvited
in someone's backyard.

I am a small brown bird,
virginal and quickly flustered.
I am the whisper of the curtain drawn shut,

the feeble alarm that sounds shriller when ignored.
At the edge of the spoiled river flats,
I will insert myself

into the ashen and ochre horizon,
with its soluble risk, to be a temporary installation,
a handprint on glass.

In the gallery of memory,
there are no neutral colours.
Only one visitor is admitted at a time.

I stop before a pencil-crayon drawing of a girl
with her black hair falling over her half-finished portrait
of a girl who depleted her options.

She's in the middle of drowning,
in her hair, a coronet of poppies, violets, forget-me-nots.
Her story is well-known

in English-speaking countries, and beyond,
in the village school where my mother, fourteen, traces
and adorns a mad daughter who escaped the net.

There's a landscape in sepia, a ferry slipping away
like a wish while my mother's gaze trails
its short-lived wake.

Domestic scenes, the viscous smear of Dad's moods,
his missed opportunities a latent underlayer
of blue. Half-finished studies, rough

with promise, ink brush birds and blooms
learned by rote like new habits
of dilution and recklessness.

A series of still lifes, but nothing
held still for us.
Among the filed, forgotten sketches

I identify the period when we broke
from our apprenticeship and the allure
of the Old Masters whose mandate

determined focal point, perspective, tropes
I allude to but cannot translate.
A distinctive style emerged,

often inconsistent, bolder,
cross-hatched tones and scribbled false starts
rejecting the veneration of influence.

Behind the non-reflective dustless acrylic,
the air has preserved our restlessness, our hands
scratching across archival, acid-free paper.

Here, a portrait of me
in the garden, tanned shoulders contrasting
emerald shade, my face in three-quarters,

giving the impression of avoiding the censure
of the viewer, as if embarrassed,
but no, I am being directed

to arrange myself towards a future.
I arrange myself into a frame as easy
to dismantle as a genre, as a pose, as girlhood.

.

III. BRIEF ENCOUNTERS

BRIEF ENCOUNTER WITH STRAW SANDALS

Qasr Ibrim, 8-9th c., British Museum

The hand that plaited this sole could be your hand,
could be mine. Could still be warm
as a dry patch of grass the sun has stalked through.
Could have just left the province behind my knees.
Could have turned into a fist, a slap.
Who wove such things to be ground into dust?
They have known your stride on the open road,
across dung-hardened fields, of your return,
and of your weariness, flung beside the bed.

BRIEF ENCOUNTER WITH A SITE OF EXCAVATION

It's fitting that what we cannot survive
will preserve us in stasis and bury us in silt
and good loam, under our sighs, our scrolling
over newsfeeds at the breakfast table, the butter dish,
bills and seasonal catalogues, the French press, the hints
that I would soon leave, that I never meant to stay . . .
weighed above us like the foundation to another house
to be scraped off until we're cherished, and blamed.

DISPLAY OF ASSORTED IRON OBJECTS

Like holding a weathered hand, supple with calluses,
as if helping your grandmother from her seat
or grazing the skin of a cratered cedar in the old grove,
but the weight is like that of a meteorite, fallen through fire.
When I hold that tempered weight, that wrought thing,
blood-scoured, inferno-born, I am quiet and dismembered
from what used me, and for what uses I was made.
The patina of forgetting. The pain no longer bright.

REPLICA OF A HOSTAGE
Jean Fautrier, Head of a Hostage, 1943-5

We're born with paper bags
for heads. They cringe like the skin
of boiling milk. They call out
like lanterns. While still soft
as caramels, salt-torn as mollusks,
they must be bludgeoned
with the butt end of whatever's
close at hand. Rolling pins, U-locks,
spare parts jam into the wax
where eye sockets and wrinkled lips
will tighten. Lessons of necessity conquer
cryptic shapes, sand down resistances,
sharpen true natures. We're helpless
regardless of outcome,
cast as tormentor, tormented.

INTERIOR WITH PLASTIC SLIPPERS AND BROKEN STRAPS

Song Dong, Waste Not, 2005

Because there are never enough mornings to last us
my mother stores what we don't use in a drawer
and the wrappings they came in, and the squeezed-out tubes
that reek of ointment and menthol and rosewater,
tucks them along with the sandals with the broken straps,
and the sets of Tupperware our aunties sold us at the family discount.
She would like to save the afternoons we drilled scales on the piano
when we came home hungry for sugar and butter sandwiches,
and the evenings around the Monopoly board when we traded property
like titled landlords, and left copies of Simone de Beauvoir
and Doris Lessing splayed like shrapnel on the blue carpet,
she would like to preserve them in the museum of our tenacity,
and retrieve them with curatorial remarks. We say to her, *enough*.
We say to her, there's no room for us to revolt, to turn about, to leave.
We would like to start again with wood parquet and an empty frame,
the way the house looked before we knew it, before we were satisfied.

What to do with the light that cannot be contained,
the woman that will not be held? What does she satisfy,
century to century? Treading on cobblestones
with her cloth shoes, then with a cigarette in hand,
black rain jacket, down a tear-stained lane in Shoreditch.
She has been traded for glazed ware, for piecework,
for her brothers, restless in school, and an island
where houses were tied down before typhoons sang.
When she glows with the knowledge of her place in time,
we see the patterns etched onto her polished brow.
When we visit her house she heats the kettle for tea
that tastes of mountain streams and creamy flowers,
we admire the single bough in its porcelain vase,
as if grace were our means of escape, not hers.

Before dawn breaks the back of the dark,
the lacquer-tappers beat their way to the groves,
where the trees are dripping with white fire.
There is a distance I cannot travel,
that would burn me. There are those called
to this kind of harvest, these choices.
I guess at the cramped lamplight,
the crude beginnings, the benches pocked
and marked as a face scarred by poison,
the dumb huddle of the artisan.
Beyond this exhibit, traffic courses
on the boulevards, where I'll turn and exit,
without grasping how such things
ripen into their present shape,
stickered with gold and mother-of-pearl
while it was raw and sticky as a wound.
It was crossed with meridians, cured and cooled
and hardened like the skin of the world.

I wanted to start from zero.
But no matter where I start, there is always
a disclosure I can't make visible.

In a red-brick house tilted on an axis
he who holds the title
of Royal Astronomer is deep in his linens.

He burned late in night's corridors.
He has little use for mornings. They belong
to his wife and his children, stirring sugar into porridge,

to the cook and the maids,
who know their place and keep to it,
though Agnes's favourite brother is at sea.

In the Octagon room she scours the windows
tall as giants from old tales, but she doesn't see
the coming hordes behind her like an upsurge,

spilling from wagons and tour buses
climbing the hill toward an invisible line,
a line drawn through time. They will straddle it,

take selfies, kiss while standing on the brass strip,
knowing it's a metaphor. But before we can arrive
or depart, there are redeemable problems.

There is the problem of knowing one's position
on a moving vessel, in relation to a fixed location.
These are problems of national interest.

They could fund a substantial life.
A royal warrant could be issued
for an astronomical observer to "apply himself

with the most exact Care and Diligence to the rectifying
of the Tables of the Motions of the Heavens,
and the places of the fixed Stars,

so as to find out the so much desired Longitude of Places
for perfecting of the art of Navigation."
The Observer takes his tea and buttered toast

and applies himself to the problem of designating
the burning fixtures of the visible firmament as they walk
across his sightlines. As another frigate is lost

and foundered due to coarse instruments,
ill-fated storms, running aground,
ignorance of coastlines, and errors in calculation,

the HMS Centurion rounding Cape Horn
but not knowing how far east or west they'd run
lost half its crew to the swells of scurvy.

"O! how we did rejoice and sing,
To see such prizes we had took,
For ourselves and for George our King,"

They hummed in the streets. There were prizes papered
to the alehouses, printed in pamphlets, £20,000
for determining within half a degree the longitude at sea

for the "Safety and Quickness of Voyages,
the Preservation of Ships and the Lives of Men,"
and "the Honour of Kingdom."

There are prizes for partitioning the world,
spinning in its imaginary cage
of tropic and meridian lines that tighten

over a border of poppies, a cash crop,
a seam of silver, an open port,
an island ceded under an "unequal treaty."

"Winner-takes-all," my father says.
But I am naïve, unused to framing our occupations
in terms of profit margins and winnings.

It requires a refracting, objective glass,
a spring-driven instrument inside a vacuum,
to resolve one's proper relation to liability and reward.

The reward will be dispensed after
a lifetime of labour. Of submissions, of proofs,
of mechanisms that account for changes in temperature

in tropical climates, that are counterbalanced,
that are unaffected by the pitching motion of a ship,
that are subjected to the appropriate trials.

Not even Men of Science are exempt
from such trials. Not Cambridge-educated, senior Wranglers,
Fellows and Presidents of the Royal Astronomical Society,

nor members of councils or holders of appointments,
nor a clockmaker and son of a Yorkshire carpenter
who for bounty or conquest

or a townhouse in Mayfair were adamant
for a more efficacious means of keeping time
than dead reckoning, then with a fix to the last sighting

of land as a means of reference.
Pick the church spire, London bridge,
Pick Margate, Gibraltar, Finisterre on a hazy dawn,

while aboard a trading vessel of oak imported
from the Colonies, treenailed and caulked
in Sheerness or Plymouth. The journey is subject

to cumulative errors of judgment
that prevented the shortest course, despite
chip logs, despite practiced hands counting out

the knotted log lines, despite the estimates
of nautical miles, fathoms, and speed.
A science offset by prayer and fear.

Fear dissolved tissue, bled gums, loosened teeth.
Men hemorrhaged from fear
when fresh rations were depleted or spoiled.

Fear bruised their sea-legs,
dip-dyed them as if into a vat of indigo,
blackly as orange pekoe, pungent as sumac.

Every hour they gazed
at a horizon blank as an empty coffer.
Every morning they woke further adrift.

Timbers caulked with death, the stink of it.
A gale couldn't blow it free from rigging lines
and mainsails of cream-coloured flax hauled in

so tightly they might've been a ghost-moth
pinned to glass, or a shroud.
Wind rattled away sleep, peace, and courage.

Below decks, there is a ticking heart
set to another reference point. There, it is the hour
of afternoon tea, of schoolchildren running home,

of the first four-petalled roses of the season.
The rest of the Commonwealth is relative.
If not Greenwich, or London, or Paris,

or Washington, or Cadiz, or the anti-meridian,
the imaginary line might've been engraved
beside my grandfather's house,

an island brokered by typhoons and banana trees,
a city on a river where timber rafts tumbled,
or across the broken spine of empire.

For the sake of travel, for workable timetables,
for reform and a set of universal standards,
for an attempt at neutrality,

for the sake of the 10:30 train sliding out
of Gare du Nord, for the sake of the safe
transport of mica, ginger, firearms, and iron ore,

for the sake of a profitable return,
let us adopt a singleness over multiplicity,
gaining or losing the sun-blown hours as we advance.

SUNRISE WITH SEA MONSTERS

J.M.W. Turner, Sunrise with Sea Monsters, 1845

Dressed in our Sunday best we came to pay
our respects but found you out to sea, with no time

to tide over. We'd hoped to chat
about the fishmonger's son, who's after capturing

the eye of the parson's daughter
with a look as pale as an uncooked filet.

We wanted to swim alongside your trawlers
and drifters, to see you through all weathers,

and to be seen. Many times you've come close
to catching us while schooling cod and Dover sole

hauling your worth in weight towards
scalloped dinner plates. We get that

your quotas are shrinking,
that you can't afford to look away.

The light burns through the lost years,
searing the shell-shocked, the daydreamers.

We've already given ourselves up. Now your turn.
We know there are men you call monsters

but we can't fathom how you tell them
apart from those creatures you defend as kin.

A mudlark squats, hands deep in the stink.
It's an uncomfortable posture.
Inside of Turner's ochre fog,
the flat-bottomed barges discharge their cargo
of sugar and barley and move lighter in the water.
I walk a little, and stoop, bringing my face close
to the smell of smoke and brine and dank basements.
The grey sand's uneasy. I only paid for pieces of the story,
for limited access to this registry of mud and silt.
The day's sweet as rainwater, no longer
coal-thick and yellowish, and those who haunt
the pilings and bridge spans can apply for membership
to the society of the lost and found.
Climb down to the foreshore at low tide
and if the timing's right, there's a chance of recovering
among the shush of pebbles and the detritus
of a thousand pilgrims that folded sixpence,
that hairpin of bone, whatever wrecked vessel
surrendering itself to the light, surrendering still,
to our catalogues of slim pickings.

We still benefit from the legacy,
from these curved vistas that lack disclosures.

The black oaks have given their notice
but no one wants to lose their carbon deposit.

The canopy isn't closed—
there's vacancies between the chaffed lakeshore

and the prairie grass, between Grenadier and Indian Road.
Since the surveyor in his frock coat clambered

to high ground and told his wife, "What a fine situation
this would be, if we had the means!"—a slow stream

has earmarked trails, reserved spots and come late
to stake them. Phase one's sold out.

The gables pitch their highest bid
while we mull over the profusion of mint and wild parsnip,

those hostile takeovers. Lilac and cherry capitulate
with frothing handkerchiefs and we withdraw

fingers from Picardie tempered glass and bottlenecks.
Plums at the apex of the pyramid are the first

to be bitten. The Chinese-owned fruit stand exacts a minimum
purchase for debit or credit, so might as well stock up

on staples. There's a minimum for stumbling
out to snap at the supermoon. Against chaffed balustrades,

poets in Little Prince T-shirts call for a safe ride home
after a night under the Bell Jar. Our incapacities sting

like that yellowjacket to the roof of my mouth,
its trails of sweetness. We're bandits waiting for the bill.

BRIEF ENCOUNTER AT THE NOODLE STALL

Wong Kar-Wai, In the Mood for Love, 2000

Not so much hunger as an answer to her body's
perpetual appeals. She defers to them without satisfaction,
the sound of her sandals as matter-of-fact as a metronome,
and her heartbeat a drum retreating down an empty road.
The noodle vendor fills another bowl with pulled strands,
seemingly endless bowls and endless strands into the night,
a night that is like a temporary encampment,
walls close as the sides of a tent, the streets steaming.
Under the lamplight she passes another neighbour
starched in his solitude, his glances brillantined,
his appetite sharpened for the moment he will lift
the briny broth and secret envelopes of meat and chives
to his lips, and swallow the mute plea inside.

INTERIOR OF A WOMAN AS A RENOVATION

You enter me like a surveyor and take measure
of each tender room, of my slated ribcage.

This cracked plaster is my flaked skin,
these windows my sore eyes and the penny nails

my knucklebones. If I could be gutted and refinished,
there might be potential in the way that light

stretches like a hand across the canvas drop cloths
draped over pine, floorboards, studded upholstery.

I'm not fastened together the way the clouds are fastened
to the turncoat wind. I'm not hinged the way a parawing

is hinged to gravity's wishes. The years slate me
for demolition. For now, shelter yourself

in this tent of sinews, in this collapsible woman.

INTERIOR, SCALE MODEL

Soon to come, to be built on the remains
of emptied foundations, a cavity of earth,
forty storeys rising above the fray and traffic,
suites for living now in pre-construction.
Its scale model glows from within, a lantern
of card stock, foam and plastic composite,
its pearlescent light the colour of a promise.
This white hive, monolith, ivory tower
of a dying moonchild, is yet absent
of our warm, bath-like nights, of our grins
and swallowed smoke, of our soft ghosts
and vestiges of conversation. Because don't we
deserve an emptied cache, a deleted search history,
a version of yourself updated and released
from the spectre of smashed glass, of removal,
of having the tea set and mahogany wardrobes
wrapped in cotton sheets   the factory dye vats
and bolts of unsold indigo   madder silk   brocade
left behind   as bribes to a new order
while my grandparents gave notice   regrouped
on a smaller scale   sent my father climbing
over cane chairs on the balcony   engaged him
behind the façade of prosperity.   I press against glass,
hear floors bending   under the weight of tiny people
see the silhouettes   bowed down   shrunk to fit

INTERIOR WITH A HUNDRED VIEWS

Song Dong, Communal Courtyard, 2011-2013

When they are shut, the wardrobe doors deny
that we ever crashed through them.

Why would we do such a thing?
They are not entrances, not vestibules.

They store bedding, winter coats, albums of pressed flowers,
necessary and unnecessary items,

that we forget when they're tucked away
behind etched mirrors and furrowed curtains.

Every family counts its cupboards, armoires, and cabinets.
Every family can be unlatched.

We hide unwanted gifts and detritus,
foreign novels and thoughts as if they'll be held against us,

as if they'll be paraded through the courtyard
and told to kneel in the snow until it's flecked red.

Inside our houses there is another house,
inside the wardrobes is a village I've never visited,

inside the drawers is a woman under a tree with pink flowers,
a view tucked in old cotton for when I will earn it.

i. Red Shoes at Rest

Gathie Falk, 18 pairs of Red Shoes with Roses, 1973

Will no longer cut across parquet of Calacatta marble,
or bisect a sidewalk laid with bins of dried fish and shrimp.
My leather soles do not remember painted foyers
or food courts competing for our appetites.
Once my stacked heels spanned bridges,
spun outside bistros, florists, subway entrances
paved with gum and milky tea, my insteps raised
above gravelled paths and into aerosolized taxis.
I have no more commutes. Grounded, my shoes
sprawl along the floor like sentries off duty.
One pair, not mine, is still in the fray,
on rumbling bus floors, sleepless escalators
and tiled floors that carry no sunrises, no twilights.

ii. Clear Schedules

Agnes Martin, On a Clear Day, #22, 1973

We separate the year of porousness
with virtuous lines.
We count our avid noons,
Bacchanalian dinners, midnights
that infected us with dissatisfaction
like a red stain, like a migraine.
We'll populate the calendar blocks
with meeting invites where we embellish
achromatic outcomes, zero-case scenarios,
fill in the cartography of boxes drawn
by a body that appears at first glance
uniform but on closer regard
publishes the shake of the lawless hand.

iii. Feedback Loop

Janet Cardiff, The Forty-Part Motet, 2001

Rumours escalate like swallows above fluted roofs,
beating slantwise to the palaces of justice.

Our acts of faith aren't worth
what they used to. We folded coins to cure

what ailed us, paid pilgrims in our place.
In the wings, the choir gathers its thoughts.

A parliament of voices releases its projections,
builds consensus by semitones and minor intervals.

The sun has changed its key, descending
its curve over a lottery of awnings and field tents.

We sight-read streets, transposed by catastrophe.
Our saints' days already spent.

A portfolio of stars predicts the next wave.
We're invested, lending an ear to each channel.

The counterpoint retrieves us like the accused,
and we stand at the centre, the swelling chorus

springing its vertical ruse, or worse,
praise we couldn't possibly deserve.

vi. Burden of Care

Shary Boyle, Burden I, 2010

I will carry you from your raised bed
to the nurses' station, from your salt bath
to the fertile village you left as a girl
and whose latitude I never had to lose.
I will bend to counterbalance your weight,
light as a cradle, your bones porcelain,
your teeth retiring its calcium.
Some insist you're less human, skin scaly,
gaze like a stag, that your needs
are voracious, hourly, that they will break
my communal back and strain
our lush resources. Still I will tote
my grievances like fantastic dolls
until my transformation, until the letting go.

v. Sunset to Sunrise Dance
Rebecca Belmore, Clay on Stone, Toronto, 2016

The clay cannot be returned to the cliff-deposits
they were raked from, nor do we have the will to,
once it's dried, fired and given over to utility.
So it has been carried here on the backside of song
by a wide woman, walking to and fro,
her feet bare and bleeding on granite tile.
We invited her into this house of the dead
so she can make another floor, skin-slick,
slapping it down like accusations, like fertilizer.
We watch it as if it might germinate, rhizomic
networks of reeds and wild rice, take back
territory for canoes and chorus frogs.
We want to witness this repatriation
but our legs are unused to the span of sunsets
so we sit awhile, borrowing her resolve.

IV. WITHOUT ELEGIES

Yes, we were awake and not yet awoken.
Yes, our routes were preordained.
Scenarios ran silver-seamed trees in our veins.
At alarms' raw flare, we somersaulted
like minnows into somnolence. Daylight ripped
holes in us that mended when we rose
wordless and eyeless. We steered ourselves
through the rubble of our bedrooms,
our mothers' pleasure and our fathers' wounded laughter
without colliding into hardwood and if we did,
bruises were stick-on tattoos, livid, temporary.
We could shepherd our brothers and sisters
out of cul-de-sacs and Bermuda grass.
We could wear the prized sun
around our necks. We could make a break for it
when told to shelter beneath our desks
as if they were the sky, raining lead
pencils and eraser dust. Will we be permitted
to change the streets into tributaries? Yes.
Permission came like a clutch of marbles,
like confetti from balconies, rewards
not for dying, but for waking.

A girl waits for permission to enter her life.
I hear her hunger like the rustle of paper,
making its own envelope.
I have been her polite heartbeat,
stored in a drawer with her calligraphy pens,
mixtapes and ticket stubs.
I have been her wet eyes across the *Dear Reader*,
her means of escape since a man downstairs
threw the doors into their frames.
In the glaze of summer evenings
she climbs onto the roof, and I have been there since.
The elm tree my father planted
the year I was born reaches its thin, coaxing arms.
At school they make us repeat what to do
if your house welcomes an inferno.
Take nothing with you. Find the inch of air
between the smoke and the floor.

without TESTIMONY

Michael Pittman, Trance Products, 2016

There are laws against this kind of roaming,
so when Dad saw you at the foot of his bed like a pillar
he couldn't negotiate, I took that he was apprehended
by the seeing, that it scoured a wide stripe in his life
pitiless as static, like a TV channel no longer broadcasting.
That we had visitation rights, which could not be
renounced, and that dragged after us from house to house
like frayed red ribbons, slippery, semblance-shod.
Once a bird, plain and mottled on the branch,
brokered a window for another sort of outside
and trespassed without any skill or instinct for assault.
It became enemies with us, with our chairs
and tables and lamps, mute and without testimony.
I asked if she was like that, before she was tame.

Some of us were permitted to hang red lanterns, others were not.
Some of us pasted slogans on rice paper in the tanked squares,
others read them. Others took pleasure in the tearing
of old scrolls, while many tucked landscapes and plum boughs
into their sleeves like arms without flesh, extra bones by their sides.
Thousands delivered their daughters to the furrows, to be adopted
by west winds. Others swaddled rosewood cabinets in cotton batting,
rooting their four legs in one-room tenements, in new territories.
A small but significant minority slipped like paddles through
sullen waves that swallowed some and not others, that sucked hungrily
at a younger son yet bore a sister to patrolled shores.
Millions saved coupons, hoarded oil, sent letters to Second Uncle
who left without a change of clothes. So-and-so's son won a scholarship.
The doctor's eldest came back to visit without an accent.
Some couldn't load the webpages. Others in the special districts
argued there could be no punishment without grounds.
Hundreds of mothers sang songs and pleaded with the officers.
A student surveyed her classmates on the new rules of surveillance.
My cousin reported the situation looked worse than it was.
Specialists assuaged that the situation was being contained.
In the new year, residents self-checked steady temperatures.
Travellers were sealed inside hotel rooms like undelivered threats.
The cleaning lady blurted on in a dialect I couldn't hold.
Anyone watching us thought it was a conversation.

without CUSTOM

Passed down like storm glass, they predicate disaster
and so we avert our eyes but not our hands.
My father senses a shape as chilly as a snowdrift and I don't ask
if it had a bluish tinge. It wasn't a matter of belief.
I was told, never offer pallid flowers to your elders.
And yet for a time, our garden was saintly with lilies,
dogwood, and apple blossom. I can't deny their transparency,
even in semi-neglect, was beyond reproach.
The sight of mourners in pale regalia sent my mother,
then a child, into speechlessness. Rules can be custom-made
but like a house must contain paper napkins, eggshells,
piano keys, porcelain, pearly rice, salt over the shoulder.
At a certain age, I stopped drawing from life,
not trusting the scenes before my eyes.

without PARADES

Dawn doesn't so much break as it relieves
night's watchmen, unties cold knots from our throats.
We rise and dress without checking the forecast,
already sensing that a half-haze will clothe the streets.
We know what will shake at our approach
down the boulevards, lined with weak-willed,
blighted chestnuts and honey locusts:
plates of rainwater will shimmer on the road,
the glass in the shop windows, boarded up
like eyes after cataract surgery, too delicate for exposure.
We'll proceed up broad-minded avenues,
fog lifting from the crowds like a blindfold.
Hand-in-hand with children so they could reserve
a trenchant legacy. They questioned us
and our transparent expressions, our barrelled mouths.
The day will entangle us like handcuffs, like zipties,
bind us with resinous smoke and our inviolable rights.

without OCCUPATION

But I have lost the red thread, the blue trail markers
affixed to pine bark, the footpath through waving grasses,
persuasive gate rattling in the breeze, as a ripple
through water, and it's true, I want to plunge into
the allure of that umber shade at the edge of the marsh . . .
                    and yet, were they ever there to begin with,
those ledges, those clearings where the light stills enough
for me to gather occasions where I meant to reveal myself,
so you might offer an interior in return, and what would I do
should I reach the end of them, and is there an end,
or would the trail merely loop back upon itself,
as if it didn't remember me, as if it ever did.
                    And what if there is no way through,
no openings through parks that maintain their calm,
through the territorial instinct of cinderblock and gutters . . .
                    but there is the drop, I see it between the reeds,
down the valley towards the recovered marsh,
and alongside the river loosening towards its mouth,
dog walkers and runners and children couched in watchfulness,
awaiting their inheritances, already clutching the full air,
the gold-yellow leaves, the stitches we put into the earth.

Every stitch the same length, my mother
maintains the uniformity of each seam.
At seventeen, her girlhood is deducted
at the end of each month. There are duties

charged to the blouses I order online,
black blouses, multipurpose, which I wear while
on indistinguishable subways towards
tutoring centres scented with milk tea

where students unpack knapsacks of expectations
sewn in Taiwan, pull up Nike hoodies
over T-shirts bedazzled in India, Hong Kong, and Turkey,
their Samsungs and iPhones sibilant as cicadas,

discomposing them before assignments requiring
an exposition of the main ideas, an analysis,
in their own words, of the stylistic features
of the avant-garde or the Italian futurists.

They disembark perpetually, tumble through customs,
declaring everything of value, polyethylene cases
rolling under the aroma of shawarma and samosas.

Their faces masked like a foggy window,
landing in waiting rooms, into first-come,

first-serve slots and appointments.
I take the stairs, am mistaken in the elevator

for a student. They swarm out in narrow columns,
tilting paper cups of French roast coffee,
acorn-coloured Fjällräven bags, and Vuitton purses.

I translate for them the slushed streets,
course descriptions, offhand comments swirling

through corridors like snow, I warn them of
flu season, their reduced immunity.

They tap on screens to receive wire transfers,
to start the wheel of downloads, to register

aspirations. Their fathers oversee
the production of health devices, calibrate settings,
and maintain the flow of exports and flash memory drives.

Whatever followed them here winds
between the excavation sites, infects the city

with cravings for hot dry noodles,
jianbing with hoisin sauce and airborne ambitions.

At 21, my mother inked mock-ups in Cooper,
Windsor, and Times New Roman. I tell the story

of correcting her copy while she scrolled over templates
until her lamp made another moon in the dark,

how she worked so that I might take a shortcut
through the campus, stammering like a beehive,

each cell a hex of efficiency and foraged sweetness,
so I might hold the door for those behind me,
toting portfolios of invested faith.

without CAPITAL

At the end of the day I total up my unspent skies.
Grey undecided ones, ones pink as conch shells

and as treasurable, touched with gold, effusive ones,
ones that stacked up its charcoal and exhaust

like towers built on columns of zeros. I must keep
something in reserve: a clearing between the beech,

and chokecherry, where ferns thicken the umbrage,
where shots of light and ample silence cost little

but a remnant of riverbank. In the spirit of saving
seamed in me by my grandmothers and relations

I am thrifty with my views of water, with lessons
of displacement, when, at the end of the season

a young fox crossed the road, looking over his shoulder
as if he were prey, not predator. As if the fading valley

were giving chase, wanting his bright fur and avidity,
while neighbors stood stock-still in leaf-thick gutters,

clutching their mixed breeds. At the lake's edge, the sun
signals that it's someone else's turn. It has always been

international. I have paid for the catastrophe of arrival.
The price is an immeasurable breath, a flight

untamed, arching over powerlines and leashed pets.
Traded without knowing what wildness is worth.

I have nothing to do with the relief
of bedrock north of Gananoque,
the chartreuse smear of lichen.
I have no house in that part of the country.
If I did, night would knock at the windows.
I would wake holding quiet in my mouth
like a brass nail I was afraid to drop,
to lose behind the stove, or among my papers.
                    Back in the city I mark plans.
My mother tells me how a house must be arranged
to stave off bad spirits. The alignment of doors,
and the four directions. She tells me dates
for good travel and potential delays.

In the year of stallings, of graceless tenancy,
pain walks across my shoulders
gouges a trail through the country of my sleep
takes residence in my blind bones.
I could be an accomplice to my disappearance
                    but I would have learn many things—
how to drive in fog and whiteout conditions,
check pilot lights, scatter mice, keep a dog company.
                    Things I already know:
how to live alone, how to arrange abundance,
how to skim the scum off a pot of soup bones,
how to fold each day inside its envelope,
how to pick up a lost stitch and to set dyes.
I have made things without knowing how I held
that knowing. If there are skills passed down
through the marrow then likely I could also lie,
cheat, steal, and bribe out of an untenable situation
the way my grandfathers did.

It is said that ghosts
cannot follow you over water though how can I know?
It's said a high forehead will disarray a demon.
It's said if you have one eye wider than the other,
you will be the one the spirits visit.
Mom bares her forehead.
Dad takes off his glasses, stares straight ahead
so we can measure. He tells us of a cold sensation
and I believe him. On our way home,
we catch the river tumbling the way it always has,
before we arrived. I breathe on the window
to know that I was warm-blooded.

There were other encounters in stairwells,
at the foot of hotel beds, at the top of the hill,
and it was not something he could see or retrieve,
only a formlessness, a white shape that left him
unable to gesture or let go.
Our house was newly pieced
and therefore had no traces or lingering whiffs,
and my parents travelled over oceans, so surely
no shades pursued them, transatlantic.

In my mother's village, we hike up the hillside
to the crescent graves, with their own little houses.
My uncles scatter leaves, retouch the characters
on my great-grandmother's headstone,
while my mother lays out glistening cha-shu and oranges,
stuffs the tiny house with paper money and clothing.
We press the incense in our palms. Mom tells us
of walking home at night, hearing the swings
creaking without wind, racing to her bunk
without looking back. She tells us of mourners
beating their heads and tearing their garments
while she, a child, was a witness
in the doorway, immobilized.

   On the day of my grandfather's funeral,
we drive up Yonge street for hours. I count the blocks
as I see them, 4500, 4600, 4800, 5000.
A street with a dragged memory, the trail cleaved by
Loyalist farmers to tote livestock to market.
The trail cut through hunting grounds,
creek mud and moraine, is now lined
with the languorous glow of bubble tea shops.
    We don't wear white banners
or wail through streets. But there is the honeyed waft
of sandalwood and camphor, and a plot
that I couldn't find alone.

That year, my mother is heavier,
sleepless with star-charts. She moves them
from house to house, writes their names in ink.
I tell her I don't want to carry
the burden of almanacs, of knowing
elements in balance, how to place bamboo
in water to draw a good life,
how to pass a candle through a house
to expel old dreads and footfalls.

I'm not willing, it's too heavy to dream
as my Dad does of the shapes cast
at the bottom of his bed, catching forgiveness.
I want nothing to trail me through the ravines.
I don't sprinkle salt behind me as I've been told.

I rise each morning not to enter
for I am already in the midst of disarray,
this afflicted world, with entrances
inside entrances inside cordoned routes.
Walking down to the river, past yards of sage,
lavender, dandelion, juniper, white spruce, and other
medicines, I pick up wind-broken boughs.
They can build resistance in the body
racked with bad winds, repair imbalances
in complement systems.
        Here on the sprung earth,
by the water that washes out the poison,
the proliferate aches lift, at least momentarily,
but not the accumulations of grief,
not the invisible war among fences and storm drains.
What exchange for a story, a rift-making, a disturbance
in depositing my trailing and voracious spirits,
in taking what is owed to me   of the gifts of futurity.

The landscape of "Night Scene for a Revoked Citizen" is that of Prince Edward County, Ontario, where I swam in Roblin Lake with friend and poet Laura Clarke at the Al Purdy House in Ameliasburg, and also at the Spark Box Studio in Picton, Ontario. During my stay there in September 2017 this manuscript had its origins.

In "For a Millennium", the line "Just once in my life, I'd like to sleep until I woke up natural" is spoken by the character of Anna Smith, head housemaid in the series *Downton Abbey* in the first episode of season one.

"For a Temporary Encampment" takes place during a large-scale installation coordinated by Thomas and Guinevere for the Luminato Festival in 2012. This installation at Fort York consisted of 200 canvas tents, each one containing a story of a real person in the region during the War of 1812. I created installations for two historical figures: Catherine Brant and Joseph Barss.

"Interlude, a Relapse, Coming to Know" refers to the phrase "Coming to Know" used by Nadia McLaren, a filmmaker and educator. I thank Nadia for her generosity in sharing her Anishinaabe teachings, which continue to inform my relations to Turtle Island.

This poem also refers to the demonstrations of solidarity and rail disruptions near Belleville, Ontario where members of the Tyendinaga Mohawk nation, activists and supporters of the Wet'suwet'en First Nations land claims in BC blockaded the CNR rail line in early February 2020.

"Nude with White Space" responds to Chinese-American artist Walasse Ting's (丁雄泉) lithographic print, *Woman with Flowers*, 1977. My father bought a print of this work at the Byward Market in Ottawa in the late 1970s that hung in our home whenever we moved.

"Still Life without Separations" has as its backdrop Henri Matisse's *Goldfish and Sculpture*, 1912. A 1978-79 MOMA exhibition poster of this painting hung in our bathroom.

"Vous savez bien que dans le fond je n'en crois rien" is from the song "Parlez-moi d'amour" written by Jean Lenoir in 1930 and sung by Lucienne Boyer. My mother remembers her grandfather listening to French records. I imagine this might be a song she heard.

"Still Life with Dream Interpretation, #2" responds to Lu Shou Kun's (呂壽琨) ink brushstroke painting, *Zhuangzi is Free*. A print of this work hung in my mother's bedroom and studio. See notes of *Admission Requirements* regarding this painting.

"Still Lives" refers to the film *Camille Claudel* (1988), directed by Bruno Nuytten and starring Isabelle Adjani.

On a family trip in New York City in 1991, my sister and I were taken to view Claude Monet's *Water Lilies* at the Metropolitan Museum. Our parents were in the habit of travelling to see touring exhibits of impressionist works, though in 1991 we were ostensibly in New York to view a Frank Lloyd Wright Exhibit.

A 2006 BBC mini-series titled *The Impressionists* provided some source imagery for this poem.

"Brief Encounter with Straw Sandals" responds to an exhibit at the British Museum of a single straw sandal from the Qasr Ibrim, an archeological region of Lower Nubia located in modern Egypt, from 8-9th c. Craftspeople in China and Japan still make sandals by hand from hemp fibre or rice straw.

"Display with Assorted Iron Implements" was a part of the British Museum Hands on Desks programme. During a visit in 2013 the museum placed a number of Iron Age tools and implements on a table in a throughway for visitors to touch and learn about.

"Interior with Plastic Slippers and Broken Straps" responds to Chinese conceptual artist Song Dong's installation *Waste Not*. The installation is made up of his mother's wood frame house and is surrounded by its contents. Dong collaborated with his mother, Zhao Xiangyuan, to display her "hoardings," objects saved during the Cultural Revolution when daily essentials were difficult to come by. Dong integrates the Chinese "Wù jìn qí yòng" (物尽其用) waste not philosophy. The installation was also a means to grieve her passing in 2009, when he remade the exhibition.

"Lacquered Bowl" responds to a 2009 exhibit at the Montreal Botanical Gardens titled "Lacquer, Precious Resin" a collection of lacquer pieces made by members of the Japan Urushi Art and Craft Association.

"Brief Encounter with the Greenwich Meridian" makes use of numerous research materials including the *Royal Observatory Greenwich Souvenir Guide*, published 2012 by NMM Enterprises Ltd. and the Royal Museums Greenwich website, and *Longitude*, a 2000 TV movie directed by Charles Sturridge on the life of John Harrison, who built the marine chronometer for navigation at sea.

The poem refers to a royal warrant issued in 1675 by King Charles II which gave the title of Astronomer Royal to John Flamsteed, appointed to "apply himself with the most exact Care and Diligence to the rectifying of the Tables of the Motions of the Heavens, and the places of the fixed Stars, so as to find out the so much desired Longitude of Places for perfecting of the art of Navigation."

The HMS Centurion was a British Royal Navy ship which in 1741 near Cape Horn was struck by a storm that lasted nearly two months, losing several men to scurvy each day. The difficulty of determining longitude resulted in the Centurion sailing west, reversing and sailing east, and reversing again once Captain Anson realized their position. The two weeks of zigzagging cost the Centurion an additional eighty lives.

The song lyrics "O! how we did rejoice and sing . . ." are from a song titled "The Lucky Sailor; or the Sailor's Invitation to Go with Admiral Anson," written in 1745. The song appears in *Naval Songs and Ballads*, edited by C.H. Firth in 1907.

The Longitude Act of 1714 was an Act of British Parliament passed during the reign of Queen Anne. It offered a series of rewards from £10,000 and up to £20,000 for anyone who could find a practical way of determining longitude at sea within certain degrees of error.

I have excerpted from the act's opening, which reads: "Whereas it is well known by all that are acquainted with the Art of Navigation,

That nothing is so much wanted and desired at Sea, as the Discovery of the Longitude, for the Safety and Quickness of Voyages, the Preservation of Ships and the Lives of Men : And whereas in the Judgment of Able Mathematicians and Navigators, several Methods have already been Discovered, true in Theory, though very Difficult in Practice, some of which (there is reason to expect) may be capable of Improvement, some already Discovered may be proposed to the Publick, and others may be Invented hereafter : And whereas such a Discovery would be of particular Advantage to the Trade of Great Britain, and very much for the Honour of this Kingdom; . . ." The full act can be read in the University of Cambridge Digital Library.

The Treaty of Nanking which ceded the island of Hong Kong, Kowloon peninsula and New Territories to the British government as well as opened up four additional treaty ports after the First Opium War in 1841 is referred to by scholars and the Chinese as an "unequal treaty."

In 1884, forty-one delegates from twenty-six countries met at The International Meridian Conference to determine a prime meridian for international use. Several meridians were in use at that time, include Greenwich, Paris, Washington, Cadiz, as well as 2881 'miscellaneous' meridians. The delegates recommended the Greenwich Meridian as the international standard for zero degrees longitude.

"Still Life with Sea Monsters" was a part of Paul Vermeerch's 2015 blog poetry project, where he invited poets to write an ekphrastic poem on J.M.W. Turner's *Sunrise with Sea Monsters*. Thank you to Paul Vermeersch for his invitation. The poem also makes use of a 2008 documentary titled "The Last Fisherman" produced by Modus Film Productions, and directed by Mark Castro.

"The Society of the Lost and Found" refers to the 'Thames and Field' club, a group of people who walk the banks of the River Thames in London searching for historical objects and finds on the shore. 'Mudlarks,' according to the Thames Museum, was a term used from the late 18th century for people who scavenged the riverbank for items to sell, many of them children. Until the 20th c. mudlarking was recognized profession.

"Landscape with Surveyors" imagines the figures of John Howard and his wife Jemina. According to the High Park Nature website, Howard was a city surveyor who purchased a sixty-six hectare lot in 1836, built Colborne Lodge and named the estate High Park.

"Interior with a Hundred Views" responds to Song Dong's installation, *Communal Courtyard,* which was exhibited at Art Gallery of Ontario in 2016. It is made of 100 vintage Chinese wardrobe doors attached together in spiraling lines. In a talk at the AGO in June 27, 2016, Dong spoke of how much he wished for one of these wardrobes, which his father had built for family members.

Rebecca Belmore's *Clay on Stone* was a performance installation which took place at Nuit Blanche in September 2016 at the Art Gallery of Ontario in Toronto. During a twelve-hour performance, Belmore applied clay to the stone floor of the Walker Court, at first writing words such as "Land" and "Water" but eventually covering the floor with patterns.

"Without Permission" is dedicated to the students, teachers, and staff who lost their lives or were injured when a student opened fire on school premises. In 2018 there was a particular concentration of these incidents in the news, at Marshall County High School, Marjory Stoneman Douglas High School, and Sante Fe High School.

"Without Testimony" was written for the launch of Ruth Roach Pierson's chapbook launch in 2016 at the Abbozzo Gallery in Toronto. Thank you to Ruth for inviting me to take part of this event. As the chapbook cover and the gallery featured the work of Newfoundland artist Michael Pittman, I wrote "Without Testimony" in response to his painting "Trance Products."

"Without Parades"
The red thread alludes to the Chinese, as well as Korean and Japanese belief of the "red thread of fate," where an invisible red thread is thought to connect two people destined to be in love.

"Without Inheritances"
According to the Richmond Hill Public Library, Yonge Street was laid out in 1794 by surveyor Augustus Jones, beginning with a post near the Toronto bay at the foot of Yonge Street and continuing to Holland's Landing. Following the survey lots of 200 acres were laid out on Yonge up to Lake Simcoe, which over the next fifty years were partitioned, sold off, cleared, settled and farmed.

ACKNOWLEDGEMENTS

Thanks to the editors of *Arc Poetry Magazine, Best Canadian Poetry 2021, Canadian Notes & Queries, Humber Literary Review, Literary Review of Canada, Hart House Review, Maisonneuve, The Fiddlehead, The Malahat Review, The Puritan, Room Magazine, Sindroms Magazine: The White Issue, This Magazine, Vallum Contemporary Poetry,* and *West End Phoenix* who published earlier versions of these poems.

"Occasional Emergencies" and "Replica with Hostage" is excerpted from a chapbook titled *Occasional Emergencies* with Odourless Press in 2013.

Earlier versions of "Nude with White Space", "Still Life without Separations," "Still Life for the Myth of Origins," "Family Portrait in Alla Prima, with Cool Tones," and "Still Lives" were published in a chapbook titled *Hanging Exhibits,* with The Emergency Response Unit Press in 2016.

Thank you to Canada Council for support during the writing of these poems.

Gratitude to Dionne Brand, Anita Chong, Kelly Joseph, Ruta Liormonas, Terrence Abrahams, Natalie Wee, Jared Bland and all the team at McClelland & Stewart.

Friends I could not survive without: Amanda Thambirajah, Joanne Leow, Laura Clarke, Canisia Lubrin, Souvankham Thammavongsa, Sanchari Sur, Shirley Camia, Puneet Dutt and Sennah Yee.

Thanks to Bob McGill at the University of Toronto, Diaspora Dialogues and to Tessa Griffin and Sarah Tsiang at Poetry in Voice for giving me opportunities to edit, teach and mentor.

Thank you to my colleagues at the Writing & Learning Centre at OCAD University for accommodating a poet's idea of hours. Thank you to the students whose talent continues to lighten and inspire, and to the readers who carry my work.

Cover image is a partial image of a painting by my father, John Ching-Yu Wang, and titled "Skyline of Cranes of Yaletown." To my mother, Josephine Wang, thank you for your stories.

This book is dedicated to all my sisters.

© Raul Modrano

PHOEBE WANG is a writer and educator based in Toronto, Canada, and a first-generation Chinese-Canadian. Her debut collection of poetry, *Admission Requirements* was shortlisted for the Gerald Lampert Memorial Award, the Pat Lowther Memorial Award, and nominated for the Trillium Book Award. She is a poetry editor with *The Fiddlehead* magazine and served as the 2021-2022 Writer-In-Residence at the University of New Brunswick.